10 x 4/08

D1505894

Coconut Kind of Day

Coconut Kind of Day

ISLAND POEMS

by Lynn Joseph

Illustrated by Sandra Speidel

LOTHROP, LEE & SHEPARD BOOKS   NEW YORK

First Edition 1 2 3 4 5 6 7 8 9 10

Library of Congress Cataloging in Publication Data
Joseph, Lynn. Coconut kind of day : island poems / by Lynn Joseph ;
illustrated by Sandra Speidel.   p.   cm.   Summary: A collection of
poems depicting the sights and sounds of the Caribbean islands.
ISBN 0-688-09119-9.—ISBN 0-688-09120-2 (lib. bdg.)   1. Islands—Juvenile
poetry.   2. Children's poetry, American.   [1. Caribbean Area—Poetry.
2. American poetry.]   I. Speidel, Sandra, ill.   II. Title.
PS3560.07754C6   1990   811'.54—dc20   90-6676   CIP   AC

Morning Songs

"Coc-a-toodle-too," from the galvanized gate.
"Whoo-too-too," from the sea.
"G'mornin' Miz Rosie," from the ebony man
 selling mangoes and papaws
 in the street.

Brother

Brother gone for a sea bath
down Mayaro Bay
swimmin' till he touch
high heaven
on a wave.

Mama

Mama gone to market
with the figs upon her head.
She wearin' her soft blue
dress for selling
with the fish 'round the hem.
Her hair is plaited neatly
in two long straps of black.
She walkin' tall in sandals
with the bamboo beads intact.
Mama look like Christmas
with red sorrel behind her ears.
She balance her wicker basket
like the Star of Bethlehem.

Miss Teacher

I hear the school bell ringin'
all the way over here.
I know the teacher waitin'
for me to appear.
"Miss, I sorry I late ag'in.
I had to feed the fowls."
Miss look me up and down
in my blue and white uniform.
"Class start at half eight sharp,"
she says.
And she try to look stern.
But Miss black eyes be smilin'
and I smile in return.

Snail Race

"Snail race at noon,"
my best friend Jasmine whispers.
"OK," I say, and duck my head.
I hope Miss didn't hear us.

'Cause Miss don't like no snail race.
She says, "Not in *my* class."
But come noontime when Miss go out
we line our snails up fast.

"On your marks, get set, and *go*!"
Me and Jasmine start the race.
And when the snails crawl off the course
we nudge them back in place.

They headin' for the finish line
when Miss comes walking in
and almost steps on Jasmine's snail.
"Watch out!" we both start yellin'.

Well, Miss don't say a word.
But boy, she do look vex.
And now she got us in these corners
standing by ourselves.

The Palet Man

"Soursop, coconut, mango, lime!"
Neville, Arjune, Jasmine and I
run down the street
to the palet man.
Count out our change
as we get in line.
Wait our turn
and *then* decide:
soursop, coconut, mango, or lime?

All Star Boys

Jasmine and me want to play cricket
with the All Star Boys
in their spanking white shirts
and high knee socks
and their cricket bats
perched like machetes
on their wide shoulders.

But the batsman says, "Girls
cahn bat no cork ball."
And everyone laughs.
The bowler hollers, "Girls
cahn knock down wickets."
And everyone screams.
But me and Jasmine dohn forget
and when we grown up we'll have
a cricket team
with no discrimination!

Coconut Kind of Day

Coconut drives with Daddy
'round the Queens Park Savannah
looking for the coconut man
in his coconut-leaf cabana
        Selling
Coconut sips with Daddy
of the sweet, cool coconut water.
Dribble down my chin as I pay
the coconut man his quarter
        for some
Coconut jelly with Daddy.
"Cut me a spoon, please,"
to eat my coconut jelly
under the coconut trees.

Pullin' Seine

Splash!	Afternoon tide roll in.
Heave!	Fishermen pullin' seine.
Come on!	Jasmine pulls me along.
Grab!	de nets like we big and strong.
Sink!	our feet deep down in de sand.
Hold!	on tight with both we hands.
Pull!	and tug and pull some more.
Show!	de fish who go win this war.
Crash!	We fall and de fish laughin'.
Grunt!	We up and pullin' again.
Wet!	and sandy through and through.
On no!	I wonder what Mama go do.
Look!	A big wave rollin' in.
Hurray!	Is now we bound to win!

Red Wonder

Rows of scarlet ibis
race across the sky
chasing the red ball sun
into the sea.

Steel Drum

Music always playin'
on my own island.
Reggae, rockers, calypso
the steelband panorama.
Long into the evening
after sun done gone
I keep on hearing the pan man
pom da de de de dom pom
sweet on that steel drum!

The Jumbi Man

The jumbi man a-comin'
with he monkey face
and iguana tail
and a shovel in he hand.
The jumbi man go eat you up
and spit you 'cross the island.

The jumbi man sing calypso
and he know all the words.
When the sun go down
and you see night come
is jumbi all aroun'.

Night Songs

"Pung-la-la," from the frog by my window.
"Shirr-ooo-ooo," from the midnight manicou.
"Ba-lo-ma," from the agouti in the yard.
"Rill-dee-dee," from the mongoose in the tree.
"Gonck-gonck," from the tatou by the pole.
"Urol-el-el," from the matapel.
"Good night," I whisper to my moonlight friends
 singing their bedtime songs to the sky.

A Note from the Author

When I was a little girl in Trinidad, I could not imagine anywhere else but my beautiful island, with it's tall coconut trees, sandy beaches, and happy sounds of steelband music. I've lived in many other places since then, but I've never forgotten the smells, sounds, and foods of my island. I wrote these poems to always remember. The scenes described are true: the coconut drives with Daddy, the snail races, the blue and white uniforms, and the music. But there may be words that are unfamiliar to those who are not from my island, and these I'd like to explain.

The *palet man* is our word for ice-cream man, whose ice creams come on sticks just like popsicles. *Soursop* is a fruit that is used to make one of our ice-cream flavors. *Pullin' seine* is when the fishermen gather on the beach to pull in the nets. Anyone may join in to help, and the children can take the small fish which won't be sold. *Jumbi man* is the name of our bogey man. Stories about jumbies are told throughout the year, and at Carnival many people dress up as jumbies. And *sorrel* is a plant used for making a sweet Christmas-time drink.

L.J.